CRAPTAILS

HE WORLD'S WORST, WEIRDEST, AND MOST DISTURBING DRINKS

CLINT LANIER & DEREK HEMBREE

CONTENTS

THE ART OF THE CRAPTAIL

You might have heard of the art of mixology. And how could you not? After all, the trend at any cocktail bar is to focus on drinks that take 20 minutes, cost $25 dollars, and need 12 different ingredients to make. That is mixology. Over the past 20 years, the movement has endeavored to pursue noble and important aims, like rediscovering classic cocktails long forgotten, or like shining the spotlight on quality ingredients. It has made celebrities out of bartenders, and even donned on these drink-slinging denizens a new name – the Mixologist.

The achievement of these aims was laudable, and those who enjoy cocktails enthusiastically embraced the early accomplishments of the mixology movement.

But the movement eventually went awry as all movements do. Aside from the intolerably long wait to get a drink, and the preposterous price tag attached to said cocktail, it has also rendered formations unnatural to humankind. While at first it was satisfied to create the perfect Old Fashioned, it has since grown bored and moved on to inventing its own abominations, like vegetable-based drinks, or smoked cocktails. Did the world really need these? Had anyone ever wondered why, after 200 years of bartending, these drinks were never popular or favored by the average drinking enthusiast?

Truly, anyone can juice a beet and then mix it with a spirit and deem it "art," but it takes a true artist to make a craptail. You might call them "crapologists." You'll find their creations at any house party on a Sunday, any fraternity get together on a Friday night, and any low-down dirty dive bar on a Wednesday afternoon.

These drinks – craptails – exist for no other reason than to make people cringe. They are disgusting, vile, nasty concoctions that are ordered or made on a dare. They are beverages so horrible, either by name or ingredient, that people still talk about drinking them years afterwards.

And we've recorded them all in this first-of-its-kind book. The book of Craptails.

We spent years scouring drink databases, the minds of bartenders, books, articles and any other resource we could find to fill these pages with true art – recipes that will make you vomit. All of these drinks – every single one – is real. We didn't invent any of them, we merely recorded them. Please don't hold us personally responsible for them.

This book is the logical conclusion to the mixology movement. It is the Omega to mixology's Alpha. With its publication the craft-cocktail movement has come full-circle into the crap-cocktail movement, and we are proud to be at the forefront.

We intend this book to be read by serious cocktail aficionados, and by those with a sense of humor. Do not read it if you're offended easily or have a weak stomach. The contents are definitely not suitable for work.

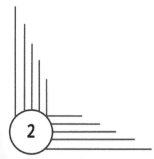

HOW TO USE THIS BOOK

Throwing your own craptail party has never been easier! These recipes can all be made in the comfort of your own home, so no need to find a fraternity kegger or dive bar to enjoy them. We've separated this book into categories of spirits and placed each craptail recipe into them, specifically: Tequila, Vodka, Whiskey, Beer, Liqueur, Gin, Rum, Brandy, and Other.

Some of the recipes call for name brand spirits, but honestly there's no need to spend a lot in making these drinks. In fact spend as little as possible. Bottom-shelf spirits work just fine in each recipe and sometimes even enhance the flavors.

You also won't need much in the way of mixers or additional liqueurs for most of the recipes found here. Craptail parties are often simple affairs and call for many things you probably already have in your fridge, like soy sauce, mayonnaise or hot mustard.

To throw a great craptail party it's important to invite your closest friends – these aren't the types of drinks to make for strangers. You also might want to think twice about using them in the company of anyone you hope to be in good standing with – so probably not a good idea to break them out for the office party or church social.

Have fun, and good luck!

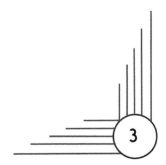

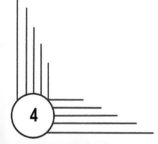

4

TEQUILA

ANUS BURNER

Difficulty Level: 2
Disgust Level: 4

1 oz. Tequila
1 slice Jalapeno
dash Louisiana hot sauce

Place jalapeno in shot glass, add tequila, add hot sauce until shot turns red and serve.

CHICKEN SHIAT

Difficulty Level: 2
Disgust Level: 4

1 1/2 oz. Tequila
1 Raw Egg

Add tequila to a rocks glass. Crack the egg into the glass without breaking the yolk and serve

DEAD GOAT

Difficulty Level: 1
Disgust Level: 4

1 1/2 oz. of Tequila
3 oz. Warm dairy (half and half preferred)

Add tequila and dairy to a rocks glass and serve.

FIRE AND TORTURE

Difficulty Level: 1
Disgust Level: 3

1 oz. Tequila
10 drops Louisiana hot sauce
5 splashes Lime juice

Add ingredients to a shot glass and serve.

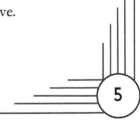

DIRTY PANTIES

Difficulty Level: 2
Disgust Level: 4

1 oz. Silver tequila
1 tsp. shredded Parmesan cheese

Pour tequila into shot glass, add tablespoon of cheese.
Serve.

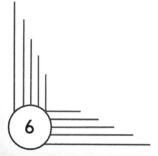

FLAT LINER

Difficulty Level: 1
Disgust Level: 2

3/4 oz. Sambuca
3/4 oz. Tequila
3 dashes Louisiana hot sauce

Add ingredients to shot glass and serve.

FOUR HORSEMEN

Difficulty Level: 1
Disgust Level: 3

3/4 oz. Tequila
3/4 oz. Jägermeister
3/4 oz. Rumple Minze
3/4 oz. Overproof/151 Rum

Add ingredients to shot glass and serve.

GASOLINE

Difficulty Level: 1
Disgust Level: 3

3/4 oz. Southern Comfort
3/4 oz. Tequila

Add ingredients to shot glass and serve.

GREASY (OR SWEATY) MEXICAN

Difficulty Level: 2
Disgust Level: 4

1 oz. Tequila
1 glob (about 1/2 oz.) Mayonnaise

Add tequila to shot glass. Squeeze mayonnaise directly into shot or onto spoon and let it slide slowly into tequila. Give it about 30 seconds to let the mayonnaise begin dissolving into the tequila. Shoot.

MEXICAN AFTERBURNER

Difficulty Level: 1
Disgust Level: 2

1 oz. Tequila
dash Louisiana hot sauce

Add ingredients to shot glass and let the hot sauce settle, then serve.

MEXICAN NAZI

Difficulty Level: 1
Disgust Level: 2

3/4 oz. Jägermeister
3/4 oz. Tequila

Add ingredients to shot glass and serve.

MEXICAN PRAIRIE FIRE

Difficulty Level: 1
Disgust Level: 2

1 1/2 oz. Tequila
dash Louisiana hot sauce

Add ingredients to a shot glass and let settle for a moment and serve.

NASTY BITCH

Difficulty Level: 1
Disgust Level: 1

1 oz. Tequila
1/2 oz. Orange liqueur

Add ingredients to shot glass and serve.

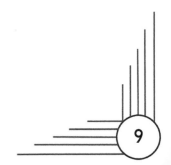

HOLY GUACAMOLE

Difficulty Level: 3
Disgust Level: 2

1 oz. Tequila
splash Lime juice
dash Louisiana hot sauce
Garlic salt
Avocado
Onion

Rim shot glass with garlic salt. Add tequila, add lime juice and hot sauce. Garnish with avocado and onion wedges and serve.

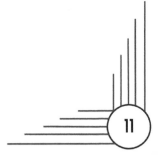

HOT MEXICAN HOOKER

Difficulty Level: 3
Disgust Level: 4

1 oz. Tequila
1/2 oz. Louisiana hot sauce
splash Canned tuna juice

Add ingredients to shot glass. Mix but don't chill, this is best served warm as a shooter.

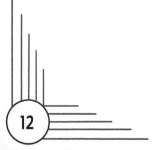

NAZI TACO

Difficulty Level: 1
Disgust Level: 2

1 1/2 oz. Tequila
1 1/2 oz. Jägermeister

Add ingredients to shot glass and serve.

SHE RAN OVER MY HEART WITH A BULLDOZER

Difficulty Level: 1
Disgust Level: 2

1/2 oz. Rum
1/4 oz. Amaretto
1/4 oz. Tequila

Add ingredients to shot glass and serve.

SPUNG

Difficulty Level: 2
Disgust Level: 3

1 1/2 oz. Tequila
1 oz. Squirt
1 oz. espresso (cold)

Add ingredients to a rocks glass and serve.

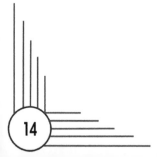

STAMPEDE BREAKFAST
Difficulty Level: 4
Disgust Level: 3

1 Raw egg (in the shell)
2 oz. Tequila
1 piece Cooked bacon
Honey

Rim shot glass liberally with honey. Add tequila. Poke holes in either end of the raw egg and place it on the shot glass. The honey will seal around the edge of the egg and the glass. Proceed to suck the tequila through the raw egg and finish it off by eating the piece of bacon.

SUCK, BAND & BLOW
Difficulty Level: 5
Disgust Level: 2

1 oz. Jacquin's Orange Flavored Gin
1 oz. Rumple Minze
2 oz. Goldschläger
1 oz. Jägermeister
3 oz. Cuervo Gold Tequila
1 oz. Hpnotiq
1 oz. Vodka
1 oz. Citron Vodka
1 oz. Triple Sec
1 Peeled whole lime
5 oz. Strawberry daiquiri mix
2 cups Cranberry juice
1 cup Sugar

Add ingredients to a blender with ice and blend. Serve in a hurricane glass.

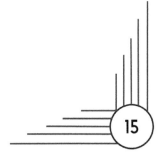

SPIC MIC

Difficulty Level: 1
Disgust Level: 2

1/2 oz. Tequila
1/2 oz. Irish cream liqueur

Add the tequila to a shot glass first, then add the Irish cream and quickly drink.

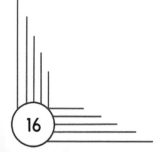

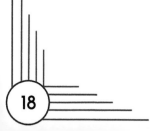

18

VODKA

ADIOS MOFO
Difficulty Level: 2
Disgust Level: 3

1/2 oz. Vodka
1/2 oz. Rum
1/2 oz. Tequila
1/2 oz. Gin
1/2 oz. Blue curaçao
2 oz. Sweet and sour mix
2 oz. 7up

Add ingredients to a pint glass and add ice. Stir and serve.

ALEATHON
Difficulty Level: 2
Disgust Level: 4

1 oz. Vodka
1 oz. Maple Syrup
4 oz. Guinness
4 oz. Coca Cola
4 oz. Red Stripe Beer

Add ingredients to pint glass. Add ice if desired. Stir and serve

BACON CHOCOLATE MARTINI
Difficulty Level: 2
Disgust Level: 3

1 oz. Vodka
2 oz. Chocolate liqueur
1 oz. Irish cream
Splash of cream
Bacon salt

Add ingredients to a cocktail shaker filled with ice. Shake well. Strain and pour into a bacon salt-rimmed martini glass.

BLACK DEATH

Difficulty Level: 1
Disgust Level: 3

2 oz. Vodka
Soy Sauce to taste

Shake soy sauce into vodka until it turns a menacingly dark
color. Serve.

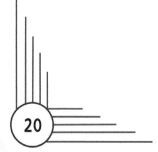

BELGIAN CAVE

Difficulty Level: 1
Disgust Level: 3

1 1/2 oz. Ouzo
1 1/2 oz. Vodka
3/4 oz. Jägermeister

Add ingredients to a rocks glass. Either shoot as is or add ice, stir and sip.

BLTINI

Difficulty Level: 2
Disgust Level: 4

3/4 oz. Vodka
3/4 oz. Tomato juice
1 dollop Mayonnaise
1/2 tsp. Bacon Bits

Add vodka and tomato juice to shot glass. Add bacon bits and top with the mayonnaise.

BLUE BALLS

Difficulty Level: 1
Disgust Level: 2

1 oz. Raspberry vodka
1 oz. Coconut rum
1 oz. Blue curacao liqueur

Add ingredients to a cocktail shaker filled with ice. Shake well, strain into shot glass.

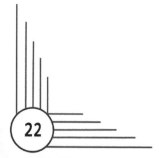

BLUE-DRIVER

Difficulty Level: 1
Disgust Level: 3

2 oz. Vodka
8 oz. Blue Kool-Aid

Add ingredients to pint glass filled with ice. Serve.

BULL SHOT

Difficulty Level: 3
Disgust Level: 2

1 ½ oz. Vodka
3 oz. Chilled beef bouillon
Dash of Worcestershire,
Dash hot sauce
Celery salt (optional)
Salt and pepper to taste

Add ingredients to cocktail shaker with ice. Shake well. Strain into pint glass filled with ice.

CHEAP SCREW

Difficulty Level: 1
Disgust Level: 2

2 oz. Vodka
8 oz. Sunny Delight

Add ingredients to pint glass filled with ice.

CHERRY BOMB

Difficulty Level: 1
Disgust Level: 2

2 oz. Cherry vodka
1 Can Red Bull

Add ingredients to pint glass filled with ice.

IMPORTED

BLOODY LEROY

Difficulty Level: 3
Disgust Level: 2

2 oz. Vodka
1/4 oz. Barbecue sauce
1/2 oz. Lemon juice
2 to 3 dashes Louisiana hot sauce
2 to 3 dashes Worcestershire sauce
Salt
Lemon Wedge
Celery Stick

Add vodka, barbecue sauce, lemon juice, hot sauce, Worcester sauce, and salt to cocktail shaker with ice. Shake well. Pour in a pint glass, stir with celery stick and garnish with lemon wedge.

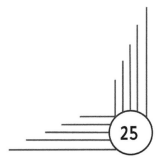

CUM IN A HOT TUB

Difficulty Level: 1
Disgust Level: 3

3/4 oz. Vodka
3/4 oz. White rum
Splash Irish cream

Add vodka and white rum to shot glass, splash a small amount of Irish cream to top. Wait for Irish cream to curdle and serve.

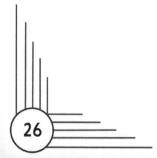

COMMANDER WHITE

Difficulty Level: 2
Disgust Level: 2

2 oz. Vodka
4 oz. Pineapple juice
1/2 oz. Lemon juice
2 to 3 dashes Hot sauce
2 to 3 dashes Worcestershire sauce
Salt to taste
Lemon wedge
Celery stick

Add all but lemon wedge and celery to cocktail shaker with ice and shake well. Strain into pint glass with ice, stir with celery stick and garnish with lemon wedge.

DIRTY POMPADOUR

Difficulty Level: 1
Disgust Level: 3

1 oz. Mandarin vodka
1 oz. Jägermeister
1 can Energy drink

Add ingredients to pint glass filled with ice.

ESTONIAN FOREST-FIRE

Difficulty Level: 1
Disgust Level: 2

1 oz. Vodka
12 drops Louisiana hot sauce
1 slice Kiwi

Add vodka and hot sauce to shot glass, garnish with kiwi wedge.

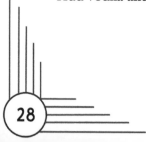

GO TO HELL

Difficulty Level: 3
Disgust Level: 4

3/4 oz. Vodka
1/2 oz. Creme de Cassis
1/2 oz. Kirschwasser
dab of Wasabi

Add vodka, crème de cassis, and kirsch to shot glass. Drop in small dab of wasabi, wait for a few moments and drink.

HEMORRHOID FEVER

Difficulty Level: 1
Disgust Level: 4

4 oz. Bourbon
2 oz. Vodka

Add ingredients to rocks glass filled with ice. Stir and serve.

HOT SPOT

Difficulty Level: 1
Disgust Level: 3

1/2 oz. Vodka
1/2 oz. Tequila
1/2 oz. Hot sauce

Add all ingredients to shot glass.

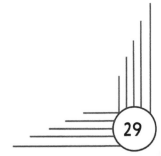

CUNT PUMP

Difficulty Level: 2
Disgust Level: 2

3 oz. Vodka
1 oz. Tomato juice
1 Tbsp. Spicy mustard
1/4 oz. Lime juice

Add the vodka and tomato juice first. Then drop in the dollop of mustard so it sinks to the bottom. Finally add lime juice. Do not stir.

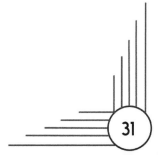

HOLOCAUST

Difficulty Level: 3
Disgust Level: 4

1 oz. Vodka
One squirt (or dollop) of hot mustard
1/2 oz. Sauerkraut juice

Mix sauerkraut and vodka, microwave for 10 seconds,
squirt in mustard and drink.

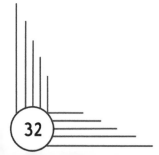

KIM JONG IL NUCLEAR BOMB

Difficulty Level: 4

Disgust Level: 5

1 Big Mac
1 large McDonald's fries
1 McDonald's tangy BBQ sauce packet
1 small McDonald's milk shake (chocolate, strawberry and vanilla mixed)
1 McDonald's apple pie
3 oz. Vodka

Add all but vodka to a blender and liquefy. Pour into glass over ice. Add vodka, stir and serve.

LIQUID BREAKFAST

Difficulty Level: 3

Disgust Level: 3

1 1/2 oz. Bacon-infused vodka

1 raw Egg, shaken until frothy

Add ingredients to cocktail shaker with ice and shake well. Strain into glass and serve.

MAD DOG

Difficulty Level: 2

Disgust Level: 2

3/4 oz. Vodka
1/4 oz. Black current cordial
1 dash Louisiana hot sauce

Add ingredients to shot glass and serve.

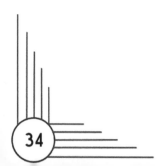

MCNUGGETINI

Difficulty Level: 4
Disgust Level: 5

6 McDonald's Chicken Nuggets
1 packet McDonald's Barbecue Sauce
1 small McDonald's Chocolate Shake
2 oz. Vanilla vodka

Add all ingredients but vodka to a blender and liquefy. Pout into glass over ice. Add vodka, stir and serve.

NYQUIL

Difficulty Level: 3
Disgust Level: 3

3/4 oz. Vodka
1/4 oz. Herbal liqueur (Chartreuse, Fernet, Jägermeister, etc.)
1/4 oz. Blue or green food coloring

Add vodka and herbal liqueur to shot glass. Add food coloring, mix and serve.

PHILLIPS SCREWDRIVER

Difficulty Level: 2
Disgust Level: 3

1 oz. Vodka
2 oz. Orange juice
1 oz. Phillips' Milk of Magnesia

Add ingredients to a cocktail shaker filled with ice. Shake well. Strain into rocks glass over ice and serve.

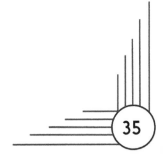

INFECTED WHITEHEAD

Difficulty Level: 2
Disgust Level: 4

2 oz. Vodka
2 oz. Bloody Mary mix
2 Tbsp. Cottage cheese

Mix vodka and Bloody Mary mix in cocktail glass, add cottage cheese and let it sit. When ready guzzle the whole thing down.

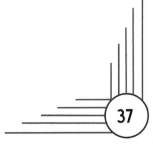

LAWNMOWER

Difficulty Level: 2
Disgust Level: 3

3/4 oz. Part vodka
3/4 oz. Wheatgrass Juice

Add ingredients to shot glass and serve

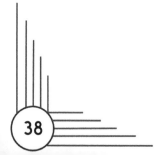

PILE DRIVER

Difficulty Level: 1
Disgust Level: 2

1 ½ oz. Vodka
3 oz. Prune juice

Add ingredients to rocks glass over ice. Stir and serve.

PLAIN PRAIRIE FIRE

Difficulty Level: 1
Disgust Level: 2

1 1/2 oz. Vodka
1 dash of Tabasco Sauce

Let the Tabasco settle a bit before shooting.

PREGNANT WIFE

Difficulty Level: 2
Disgust Level: 3

3/4 oz. Peanut butter vodka
3/4 oz. Pickle juice

Add ingredients to shot glass and serve.

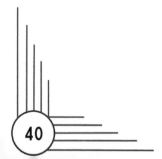

PUSSY PUNCH
Difficulty Level: 2
Disgust Level: 2

2 oz. Burnetts orange vodka
2 oz. Peach Schnapps
1 oz. Barcardi Limon
2 oz. orange juice
2 oz. cranberry juice
2 oz. 7-up
2 cherries
1 Orange wedge

Add vodka, schnapps, and Bacardi into cocktail shaker with ice. Shake well. Strain into pint glass over ice. Add orange juice, cranberry juice and 7-Up. Stir and serve. Garnish with cherries and orange slice.

ROBITUSSIN
Difficulty Level: 2
Disgust Level: 3

1 1/2 oz. Cherry Vodka
1 1/2 oz. Root Beer Schnapps

Add ingredients to rocks glass without ice. Stir and serve.

SANITIZER
Difficulty Level: 3
Disgust Level: 3

1 oz. Vodka
1 oz. White rum
3/4 oz. Lychee liqueur
3/4 oz. Cherry brandy
3/4 oz. Grenadine

Add ingredients to a cocktail shaker filled with ice. Shake well. Strain into rocks glass over ice.

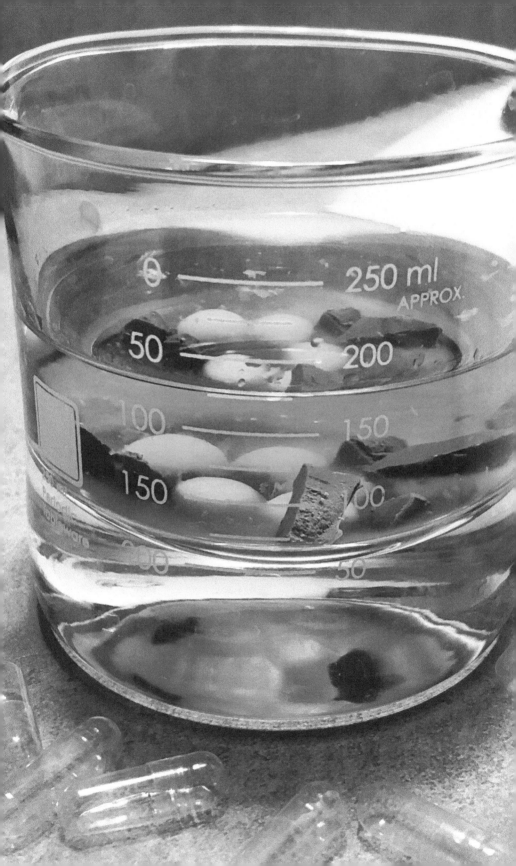

STOMACH CONTENTS

Difficulty Level: 4
Disgust Level: 4

2 oz. Vodka
1 oz. Absinthe
Chunks of chocolate
Skittles
Empty pill casings for garnish

Add vodka and absinthe to cocktail shaker with ice. Shake well. Strain into rocks glass or glass beaker (no ice). Drop in small chunks of chocolate and Skittles. Let sit to allow the chocolate and Skittles to begin to dissolve. Serve and sprinkle empty pill casings around glass.

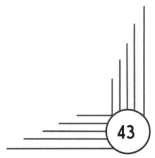

SLOE COMFORTABLE SCREW UP AGAINST THE WALL

Difficulty Level: 2
Disgust Level: 1

1 oz. Sloe gin
1 oz. Vodka
1 oz. Southern Comfort
3 oz. Orange juice
splash of Galliano

Add ingredients to cocktail shaker filled with ice. Shake well. Strain over ice in rocks glass.

SPLIFF SHOT

Difficulty Level: 3
Disgust Level: 3

1 oz. Mary Jane Vodka
1 oz. Ivanabitch Tobacco Flavored Vodka

Add ingredients to shot glass and serve.

STOOL SAMPLE

Difficulty Level: 3
Disgust Level: 3

1 oz. Vodka
2 oz. Coffee liqueur
1 oz. Cream liqueur
1 Tbsp. Cocoa
1/2 oz. Strawberry syrup
Large pieces of fudge brownies

Add vodka, coffee liqueur, cream liqueur, cocoa, and strawberry syrup to a cocktail shaker with ice. Shake well. Strain into a Ziploc plastic bag. Add brownie pieces and serve.

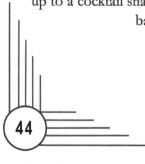

SUSHI-TINI
Difficulty Level: 4
Disgust Level: 4

1 oz. Salmon vodka
1 1/2 oz. Wasabi vodka
1 oz. Rice milk
1 sheet Sushi Nori
Pickled ginger
Wasabi

Muddle Nori in a cocktail shaker. Add ice. Add vodkas and rice milk. Shake well. Strain into a chilled martini glass. Garnish with ginger and wasabi.

THE LOX, BAGEL, AND CREAM CHEESE
Difficulty Level: 3
Disgust Level: 3

2 oz. Smoked salmon vodka
1 tsp. Capers
1 oz. Tomato juice
Splash of heavy cream
Pepper to taste

Add ingredients to rocks glass filled with ice. Stir well. Garnish with a bagel.

THE MUMMY
Difficulty Level: 1
Disgust Level: 1

2 oz. Vodka
1 oz. Triple sec
1 tsp. Lemon juice
Club soda

Add vodka, triple sec, lemon juice to a rocks glass. Fill with ice and stir. Top with club soda.

TAPEWORM SHOT

Difficulty Level: 2
Disgust Level: 4

1 oz. Vodka
1/2 oz. Hot sauce
1 squirt Mayonnaise
1 dash pepper

The vodka should be room temperature. Add vodka and Hot sauce, squirt in decent amount of mayonnaise and then dash of pepper. Let it settle for a moment and then shoot.

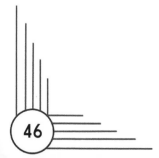

THE S.T.D.

Difficulty Level: 1
Disgust Level: 2

5 oz. Cranberry juice
5 oz. Orange juice
1/2 oz. Southern Comfort
1 oz. Vodka
1/2 oz. Jägermeister

Add all ingredients to a pint glass filled with ice. Stir and serve.

WELLEET BEACHCOMBER OYSTER SHOT

Difficulty Level: 3
Disgust Level: 2

3/4 oz. Vodka
1 freshly shucked Wellfleet oyster
Pepper to taste
1/2 tsp. Horseradish
1 dash Worcestershire sauce
1 dash Louisiana hot sauce

Add oyster to shot glass. Add pepper, horseradish, Worcestershire, and hot sauce. Top with ice cold vodka and serve.

WINDEX

Difficulty Level: 1
Disgust Level: 3

1 oz. Blue Curacao
1 oz. Vodka
1 oz. Rum
1 oz. Lime juice

Add ingredients to rocks glass filled with. Stir and serve.

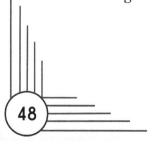

1-900-FUK-MEUP

Difficulty Level: 2
Disgust Level: 3

1/2 oz. Absolut Kurant
1/2 oz. Grand Marnier
1/2 oz. Chambord
1/4 oz. Midori
1/4 oz. Coconut rum
1/4 oz. Amaretto
1/4 oz. Cranberry juice
1/4 oz. Pineapple juice

Add all ingredients to a rocks glass filled with ice. Stir and serve.

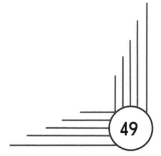

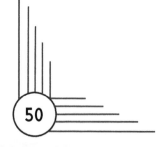

WHISKEY

ANAL INFERNO
Difficulty Level: 1
Disgust Level: 2

1/2 oz. Wild Turkey
1/2 oz. Overproof rum
1/2 oz. Jack Daniel's
1/2 oz. Louisiana hot sauce
sprinkle of pepper

Add ingredients to shot glass and serve.

BLACK SUNDAY
Difficulty Level: 1
Disgust Level: 3

1 oz. Everclear
1 oz. Wild Turkey 101 Proof Bourbon
Black cherry soda to taste

Add ingredients to rocks glass filled with ice. Stir and serve.

BUFFALO SWEAT
Difficulty Level: 1
Disgust Level: 2

1 oz. Bourbon
1/2 oz. Hot sauce

Add ingredients to shot glass and serve.

BRASS HAMMER
Difficulty Level: 1
Disgust Level: 3

1 oz. Jack Daniel's
1 oz. Tequila
1 oz. Crown Royal Canadian Whiskey

Add ingredients to a rocks glass without ice and serve.

CHARRED REMAINS

Difficulty Level:
Disgust Level:

1 oz. Jack Daniels
1 oz. Vodka
6 oz. Tomato juice
1 dash Louisiana hot sauce
1 dash Worcestershire sauce
4-5 well-cooked strips of meaty bacon
1 tsp. Sugar
1 tsp. Salt
1 dash White pepper
1 dash Paprika
Black food coloring
1 Lemon wedge

Add Jack Daniels, vodka and tomato juice to pint glass over ice. Stir well. Add hot sauce, Worcestershire sauce white pepper and paprika and stir. Combine sugar and salt in a bowl and add a few drops of black food coloring and mix until sugar and salt are black. Dredge over rim of glass. Add bacon to top of drink so it sticks out of top of glass. Add lemon wedge and serve.

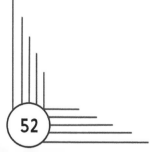

DIRTY OLIVE LEMONADE

Difficulty Level: 2
Disgust Level: 2

2 oz. Scotch
4 oz. Lemonade
2 Olives
1 Cocktail onion

Add Scotch and lemonade to cocktail shaker filled with ice. Shake well. Strain into martini glass. Add olives and onion and serve.

DUCK FART

Difficulty Level: 3
Disgust Level: 2

1/2 oz. Coffee liqueur
1/2 oz. Irish cream liqueur
1/2 oz. Whiskey

Layer ingredients in a shot glass in the following order: Coffee liqueur at the bottom, Irish cream liqueur in the middle, whiskey on top, then serve.

GORILLA'S PUKE

Difficulty Level: 1
Disgust Level: 2

1 oz. Wild Turkey 101 proof Bourbon Whiskey
1 oz. Overproof rum

Add ingredients to shot glass and serve.

Note: Can be lit and drank through a straw.

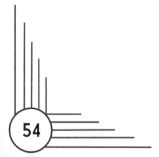

HOOKER WITH A PENIS

Difficulty Level: 2

Disgust Level: 3

4 oz. Jack Daniel's Whiskey

2 oz. Sour apple schnapps

6 oz. Coca-Cola

Add ingredients to a rocks glass filled with ice. Stir and serve.

IRISH BLOW JOB

Difficulty Level: 1

Disgust Level: 1

1 1/2 oz. Irish whiskey

1 Can of compressed whipped cream

Add Irish whiskey to shot glass. Fill mouth with whipped cream and take a shot.

MINDBENDER

Difficulty Level: 2

Disgust Level: 2

1/4 oz. Bourbon

3/4 oz. Chambord

Add ingredients to shot glass and serve.

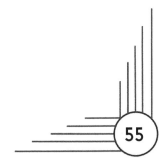

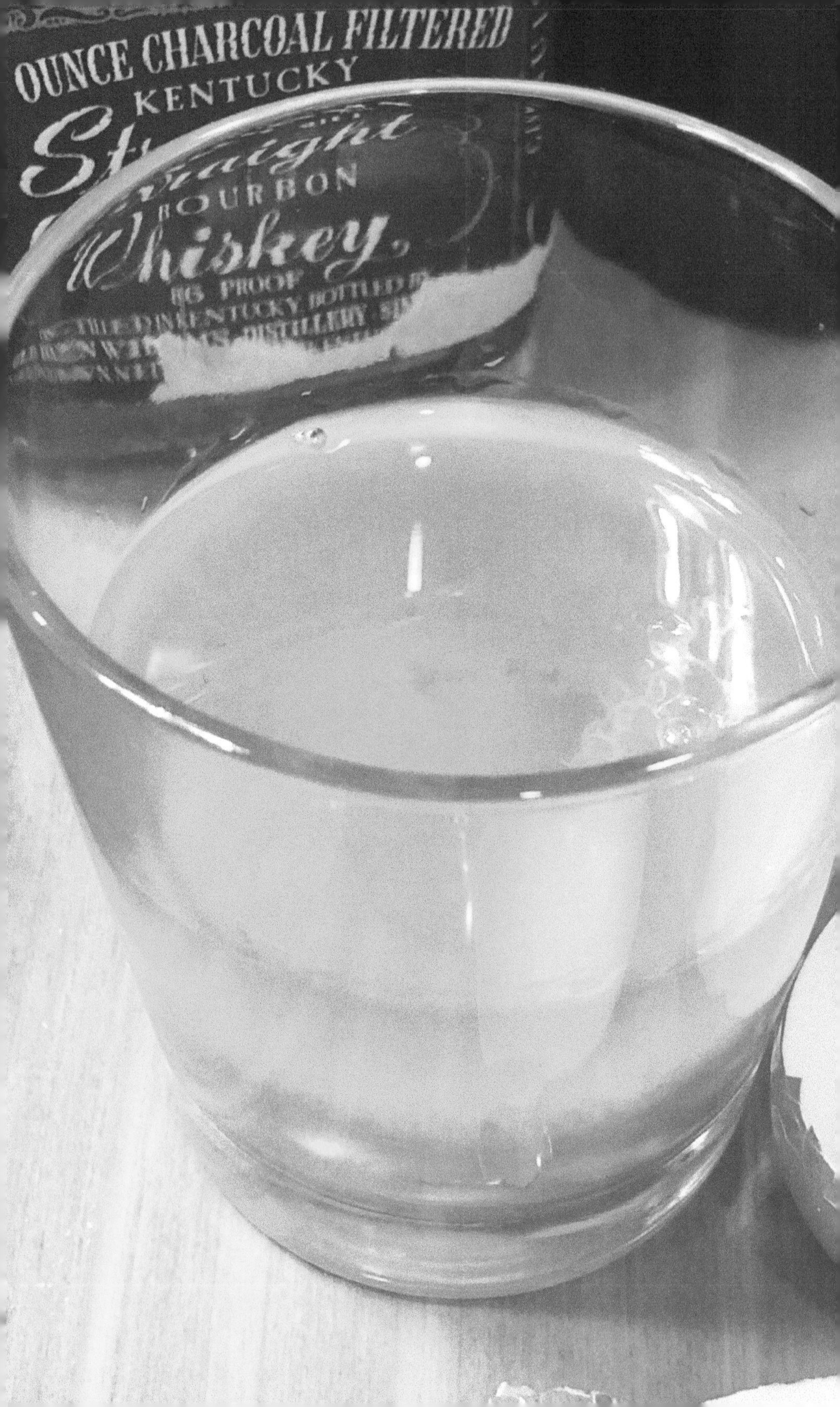
OUNCE CHARCOAL FILTERED
KENTUCKY
BOURBON
PROOF

PRAIRIE OYSTER

Difficulty Level: 2
Disgust Level: 3

1 1/2 oz. Bourbon
1 uncooked egg
1 dash Louisiana hot sauce

Pour unchilled Bourbon into cocktail glass. Add raw egg and then top with dash of Tabasco sauce. Slam immediately otherwise the egg begins to curdle.

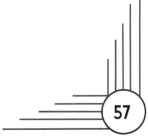

NUCLEAR RAINBOW
Difficulty Level: 2
Disgust Level: 3

1/2 oz. Grenadine
1/2 oz. Rumple Minze
1/2 oz. Jägermeister
1/2 oz. Midori
1/2 oz. Crown Royal Canadian Whiskey
1/2 oz. Bacardi Gold Rum
1/2 oz. Amaretto

Add ingredients to cocktail shaker filled with ice. Shake well. Strain into cocktail glass. Alternatively add to rocks glass with no ice as a shot.

RED NECK PRAIRIE FIRE
Difficulty Level: 1
Disgust Level: 2

1 1/2 oz. Whiskey
4 drops Tabasco Sauce

Make sure the whiskey is room temperature. Add the Tabasco and let it settle for just a bit before shooting.

REIGN IN BLOOD
Difficulty Level: 4
Disgust Level: 4

1 1/2 oz. Pig's Nose Scotch
3/4 oz. Blood orange juice
3/4 oz. Combier Roi René Rouge cherry liqueur
1/2 oz. Creme de cacao
1/4 oz. Averna amaro
1 oz. Black cold-pressed coffee
Pig's blood, for the rinse

Add everything but the pig's blood to a glass filled with ice and stir. Rinse a chalice with the pig's blood. Pour off excess blood and strain the drink into the chalice.

ROCKY MOUNTAIN BULL FUCKER

Difficulty Level:
Disgust Level:

1/4 oz. Jack Daniel's
1/4 oz. JohnnieWalker
1/4 oz. Jose Cuervo
1/4 oz. Louisiana sauce

Add all ingredients to a shot glass and serve.

RUSTY NAIL

Difficulty Level: 2
Disgust Level: 2

1 oz. Scotch
1 oz. Drambuie

Add ingredients to shot glass and serve.

SAMURAI JACK

Difficulty Level: 2
Disgust Level: 2

1 oz. Jack Daniel's
1 oz. Sake

Add ingredients to rocks glass filled with ice. Stir and serve.

SATAN'S REVENGE

Difficulty Level: 2
Disgust Level: 3

1/4 oz. Jack Daniel's
1/4 oz. Jose Cuervo
1/4 oz. Goldschläger
1/4 oz. Louisiana hot sauce

Add ingredients to shot glass and serve.

THE BLOODY TAMPON

Difficulty Level: 2
Disgust Level: 3

1 1/2 oz. Whiskey
1 1/2 oz. Tequila
1 1/2 oz. Vodka
1 oz. Vegetable juice
1 oz. Irish cream
1/2 oz. Lemon juice
1 Tampon

Add whiskey, tequila and vodka to cocktail shaker filled with ice. Shake well. Strain into rocks glass. Add room temperature tomato juice without mixing, strain Irish cream on top and splash/squirt lemon juice into Irish cream to curdle. Garnish with tampon.

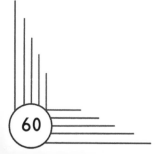

SEX ON MY FACE

Difficulty Level: 2
Disgust Level: 2

1/2 oz. Canadian whiskey
1/2 oz. Coconut rum
1/2 oz. Peach liqueur
1/2 oz. Banana liqueur
splash Cranberry juice
splash Pineapple juice
splash Orange juice

Add ingredients to rocks glass filled with ice. Stir and serve.

SPICY SANDSTORM

Difficulty Level: 1
Disgust Level: 3

1 oz. Scotch
1 oz. Gin
dash Black pepper
splash Hot sauce

Add ingredients to shot glass and serve.

SWANIE SHOT

Difficulty Level: 2
Disgust Level: 4

1 1/2 oz. Whiskey
1 1/2 oz. Milk
Raw egg

Add whiskey and milk to rocks glass. Top with raw egg and serve.

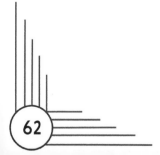

THREE HICKS AND A SPIC

Difficulty Level: 1
Disgust Level: 3

1/4 oz. Jack Daniel's
1/4 oz. Jim Beam
1/4 oz. Johnnie Walker
1/4 oz. Jose Cuervo

Add ingredients to shot glass and serve.

THREE WISE MEN

Difficulty Level: 1
Disgust Level: 3

1/3 oz. Jack Daniel's
1/3 oz. Jim Beam
1/3 oz. Johnnie Walker

Add ingredients to shot glass and serve.

THREE WISE MEN ON A TURKEY HUNT IN SOUTHERN MEXICO

Difficulty Level: 2
Disgust Level: 4

1/4 oz. Jim Beam
1/4 oz. Jack Daniel's
1/4 oz. Spiced rum
1/4 oz. Wild Turkey 101 Proof Bourbon
1/4 oz. Southern Comfort
1/4 oz. Tequila

Add ingredients to shot glass and serve.

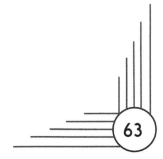

Name ⎯⎯⎯⎯⎯⎯⎯⎯⎯⎯⎯

Date ⎯⎯⎯⎯⎯⎯ Time ⎯⎯⎯⎯

Room No. ⎯⎯⎯⎯⎯⎯⎯⎯⎯

Doctor ⎯⎯⎯⎯⎯⎯⎯⎯⎯

URINE COCKTAIL

Difficulty Level: 2

Disgust Level: 3

1 oz. Whiskey

1 oz. Brandy

1 oz. Limoncello

Add ingredients to rocks glass (or urine sample jar) filled with ice. Stir and serve.

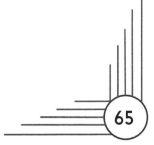

THE WHIGILA
Difficulty Level: 1
Disgust Level: 3

1/2 oz. Whiskey
1/2 oz. Gin
1/2 oz. Tequila

Add ingredients to shot glass and serve.

TURKEY FART
Difficulty Level: 1
Disgust Level: 2

1/2 oz. Wild Turkey 101 Proof Bourbon
1/2 oz. Bacardi 151 Rum
1/2 oz. Louisiana hot sauce

Add ingredients to shot glass and serve.

TURKEY SHIT
Difficulty Level: 1
Disgust Level: 2

1 1/2 oz. Wild Turkey 101 Proof Bourbon
6 oz. Tahitian Treat (fruit punch soda)

Add ingredients to rocks glass filled with ice. Stir and serve.

WHISKEY BURGER
Difficulty Level: 3
Disgust Level: 2

3 oz. Ground-chuck-infused whiskey
2 tsp. Tomato syrup
1/4 oz. tsp. Mustard bitters

Add ingredients to rocks glass filled with ice. Stir and serve.

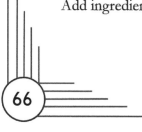

352

Difficulty Level: 1
Disgust Level: 3

1/3 oz. Bourbon
1/3 oz. Bacardi 151 Rum
1/3 oz. Vodka

Add ingredients to a shot glass and serve.

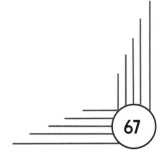

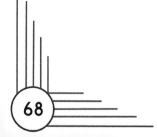

BEER

BIG FOOT

Difficulty Level: 2
Disgust Level: 2

1 Pint Beer
1 Tbsp. Honey
1 1/2 oz. Tequila

Warm honey in microwave. Add to beer. Stir. Sip Tequila, hold in mouth and guzzle beer.

BLOODY AWFUL

Difficulty Level: 2
Disgust Level: 4

1/2 pint Lager
2 oz. Vodka
8 oz. Tomato juice

Add ingredients to pint glass filled with ice. Stir and serve.

CAESAR BOMB

Difficulty Level: 2
Disgust Level: 3

1/2 oz. Tequila
1/2 oz. Hot Sauce
1 pint Beer

Add tequila and hot sauce to shot glass. Drop shot glass in beer and drink.

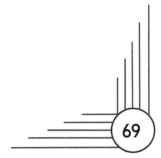

HORSE JIZZ

Difficulty Level: 1
Disgust Level: 1

12 oz. Beer (bitter or lager)
12 oz. Chilled milk

Add ingredients to a large mug and stir lightly. For a more realistic experience classic recipes call for it to be served warm or room temperature.

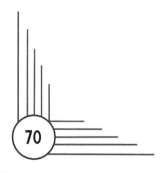

HILLBILLY LEMONADE
Difficulty Level: 2
Disgust Level: 3

3 cans Cheap beer
12 oz. Frozen lemonade concentrate
12 oz. Vodka

Add beer and frozen lemonade concentrate to pitcher and stir. Fill frozen lemonade concentrate container with vodka and add to pitcher. Stir and serve over ice.

MULLIGAN COCKTAIL
Difficulty Level: 2
Disgust Level: 2

4 oz. Beer
1 oz. Absolut Peppar

Add ingredients together into glass. Stir and serve.

PABST BLUE BALLBUSTERS
Difficulty Level: 1
Disgust Level: 3

12 oz. Pabst Blue Ribbon
2 oz. Monarch 100 proof vodka
2 dashes Louisiana hot sauce

Add ingredients to a pint glass. Stir and serve.

SUBWAY COCKTAIL
Difficulty Level: 2
Disgust Level: 3

6-16 oz. Beer remnants
1 Mulligan Cocktail

Add whatever beer happens to be around (remnants at bottom of cans, etc.) to a Mulligan Cocktail (see above) and serve.

THE QUANTUM LEAP

Difficulty Level: 2
Disgust Level: 4

16 oz. Pabst Blue Ribbon
1 oz. Vodka
1 oz. Jack Daniels
6 oz. Red Bull

Add ingredients to large glass. Stir and serve.

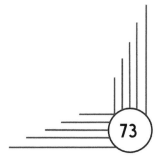

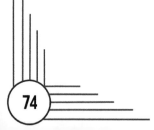

LIQUEUR

AFTERBIRTH
Difficulty Level: 2
Disgust Level: 3

1/2 oz. Irish cream liqueur
1/2 oz. Raspberry schnapps
1/2 oz. Grenadine

Add raspberry schnapps and grenadine to a shot glass. Add Irish cream and wait for it to curdle, then serve.

ALLIGATOR SPERM
Difficulty Level: 2
Disgust Level: 3

1/2 oz. Midori melon liqueur
1/2 oz. Pineapple juice
1 tsp. Heavy cream

Add Midori and pineapple juice to a shot glass. Top with cream and serve.

ANGEL'S TIT
Difficulty Level: 2
Disgust Level: 1

1/4 oz. Creme de cacao
1/4 oz. Maraschino liqueur
1/4 oz. Heavy cream
Maraschino cherry

Layer ingredients in a shot glass in above order. Chill for 30 minutes and then garnish with a cherry and serve.

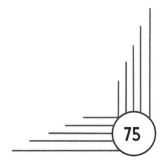

BLOATED WHALE

Difficulty Level: 2
Disgust Level: 5

1 1/2 oz. Blue Curacao
1 1/2 oz. Vinegar
1 1/4 oz. Hot sauce

Add ingredients to glass and serve.

BOBBY DAZZLER

Difficulty Level: 1
Disgust Level: 3

1/2 oz. Aftershock
1/2 oz. Tequila
1/2 oz. Whiskey

Add ingredients to shot glass and serve.

BOURBON TREAT

Difficulty Level: 2
Disgust Level: 3

1/3 oz. Blue Curacao
1/3 oz. Goldschläger
1/3 oz. Jägermeister
1/3 oz. Ouzo
1/3 oz. Rumple Minze
1/3 oz. Bourbon

Layer in a 2-ounce shot glass in the given order and serve.

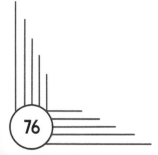

BRAIN TUMOR

Difficulty Level: 2
Disgust Level: 2

1 oz. Peach schnapps
Irish cream liqueur
Grenadine
Cherry brandy

Add the peach schnapps into the shot glass. Carefully layer the Bailey's in on the side of the glass, to almost full. Add a touch of grenadine down the middle and a touch of cherry brandy down the middle.

BUZZARD'S BREATH

Difficulty Level: 1
Disgust Level: 2

1/2 oz. Amaretto almond liqueur
1/2 oz. Coffee liqueur
1/2 oz. Peppermint schnapps

Add ingredients to shot glass and serve.

DEAD NAZI

Difficulty Level: 1
Disgust Level: 2

3/4 oz. Jägermeister
3/4 Rumple Minze

Add ingredients to shot glass and serve.

CEMENT MIXER

Difficulty Level: 1
Disgust Level: 2

3/4 oz. Irish cream liqueur
3/4 oz. Lime juice

Add ingredients to shot glass and serve.

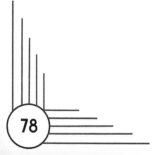

LIQUID VIAGRA

Difficulty Level: 1
Disgust Level: 3

1 1/2 oz. Jägermeister
4 oz. Red Bull

Add ingredients to glass filled with ice and serve.

MOTOR OIL

Difficulty Level: 1
Disgust Level: 3

1 oz. Jägermeister
1/2 oz. Peppermint schnapps
1/2 oz. Goldschläger
1/2 oz. Coconut rum

Add ingredients to shot glass and serve.

MOUNTAIN DEW ME

Difficulty Level: 1
Disgust Level: 2

2 oz. Midori
1 oz. Triple sec
4 oz. Pineapple juice
Splash Mountain Dew

Add first three ingredients to rocks glass filled with ice. Stir. Top with splash of Mountain Dew and serve.

PHLEGM

Difficulty Level: 2
Disgust Level: 2

1 oz. Irish cream liqueur
1 oz. Mountain Dew

Add ingredients to shot glass and serve.

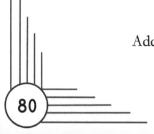

PINK PENICILLIN

Difficulty Level: 2
Disgust Level: 2

1/3 oz. 99 Bananas
1/3 oz. Midori
1/3 oz. Half and half
Grenadine

Add first three ingredients to shot glass. Top with grenadine and serve.

RED-HEADED SLUT

Difficulty Level: 1
Disgust Level: 2

1 oz. Jägermeister
1 oz. Peach schnapps
2 oz. Cranberry juice

Add ingredients to cocktail shaker filled with ice. Shake well. Strain into rocks glass and serve.

RELISHIOUS

Difficulty Level: 2
Disgust Level: 4

1 1/2 oz. Jägermeister
Sweet pickle relish

Add Jägermeister to shot glass. Top with a dollop of pickle relish and serve.

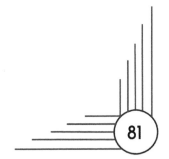

MONKEY BRAIN

Difficulty Level: 2
Disgust Level: 2

1 1/2 oz. Apple schnapps
Irish cream liqueur

Add apple schnapps to shot glass. Pour a small amount of Irish cream liqueur to top and serve.

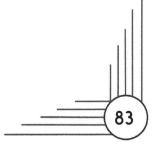

SEX WITH AN ALLIGATOR

Difficulty Level: 3
Disgust Level: 2

1/2 oz. Raspberry liqueur
1 oz. Melon liqueur
2 oz. Sweet and sour mix
1/2 oz. Jägermeister

Add melon liqueur and sweet and sour mix to a cocktail shaker filled with ice. Shake well. Strain into a martini glass. Add raspberry liqueur and top it off with Jägermeister.

SQUASHED FROG

Difficulty Level: 3
Disgust Level: 2

1/2 oz. Midori
1/2 oz. Avocaat
1/2 oz. Irish cream liqueur
splash Grenadine

Add first three ingredients, in order, to shot glass. Top with grenadine and serve.

TASTES LIKE BURNING

Difficulty Level: 2
Disgust Level: 3

1 1/2 oz. Rumple Mintze
Habanero hot sauce

Add Rumple Mintze to shot glass. Add 10 drops of habanero hot sauce and serve.

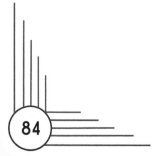

THE ABORTION
Difficulty Level: 2
Disgust Level: 3

1 oz. White creme de cacao
1 oz. Amaretto liqueur
1 oz. Irish cream liqueur
splash Grenadine syrup

Add creme de cacao into a shot glass. Layer the amaretto and then the Irish cream to create a 3 layer drink. Insert a toothpick to the bottom of the shot glass and dribble some grenadine so it floats in the bottom of the glass and then serve.

THE AXIS POWERS
Difficulty Level: 1
Disgust Level: 3

1/2 oz. Jägermeister
1/2 oz. Sake
1/2 oz. White or red wine

Add ingredients to shot glass and serve.

THE LAKER GIRL
Difficulty Level: 2
Disgust Level: 2

4 oz. Grape liqueur
4 oz. Flat Mountain Dew

Add to a highball glass and wait - the ingredients will separate into two distinct layers of purple and yellow.

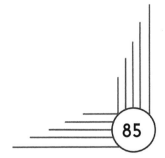

SMOKER'S COUGH

Difficulty Level: 1
Disgust Level: 4

1 1/2 oz. Jägermeister
1 tsp. Mayonnaise

Add Jägermeister to shot glass. Top with teaspoon of mayonnaise and serve.

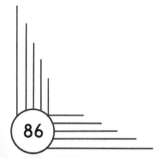

TRAIN WRECK

Difficulty Level: 1
Disgust Level: 3

1/4 oz. Irish cream liqueur
1/4 oz. Goldschlagger,
1/4 oz. Jägermeister,
1/4 oz. Rumple Minze

Add all ingredients to a shot glass and serve.

VD

Difficulty Level: 2
Disgust Level: 3

3/4 oz. Irish cream liqueur
3/4 oz. Crème de menthe
splash Louisiana hot sauce

Add Irish cream and crème de menthe to shot glass. Splash hot sauce to top and serve.

YETI

Difficulty Level: 2
Disgust Level: 2

1 oz. Jägermeister
1 oz. Peppermint schnapps

2 oz. Milk

Add ingredients to rocks glass filled with ice. Stir and serve.

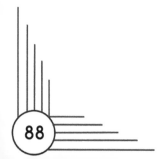

GIN

BLOODY HOOT
Difficulty Level: 1
Disgust Level: 3

1/2 oz. Gin
1/2 oz. Bourbon
1/2 oz. UV Cherry vodka

Add ingredients to shot glass and serve.

BLOODY MURDER
Difficulty Level: 3
Disgust Level: 1

2 oz. Gin
4 oz. Tomato Juice
1/2 oz. Lemon Juice
2 to 3 dashes Black Vinegar
1/8 tsp. Wasabi
Salt
Lemon Wedge
Celery Stick

Add first five ingredients to cocktail shaker filled with ice and shake once. Pour with ice into pint glass. Add salt to taste. Garnish with lemon wedge, stir with celery stick and serve.

DAWA
Difficulty Level: 2
Disgust Level: 1

1 oz. Gin
1 oz. Vodka
1 oz. Lemon juice
1 tsp. Sugar
1 Sugar cane stick

Add ingredients to a highball glass and stir over ice. Stir with sugar cane stick and serve.

PRAIRIE CHICKEN

Difficulty Level: 2
Disgust Level: 3

1 oz. Gin
1 Raw egg
dash Salt
dash Pepper

Add gin to glass of your choice (rocks, wine, martini). Crack open egg on top of gin without breaking yolk. Add salt and pepper and serve.

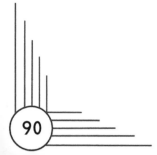

DOG'S COCK

Difficulty Level: 1
Disgust Level: 3

16 oz. Beer
4 oz. Gin

Add ingredients to tall glass and serve.

DOG'S NOSE

Difficulty Level: 1
Disgust Level: 4

2 oz. Gin
3 oz. Beer

Add ingredients to rocks glass and serve.

DRAGON'S BLOOD

Difficulty Level: 2
Disgust Level: 4

1 oz. Gin
1 packet Chinese mustard

Add gin to shot glass. Squirt in Chinese mustard and serve.

GRANDMA'S ASS SWEAT

Difficulty Level: 2
Disgust Level: 4

1 oz. Gin
1 oz. Bacardi 151 rum
12 oz. Old English Malt Liquor
splash Dr. Pepper

Add first three ingredients to chilled glass. Splash with Dr. Pepper and serve.

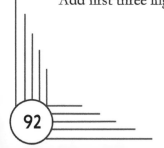

ROTTEN COONT

Difficulty Level: 3
Disgust Level: 4

1 oz. Gin
1/2 oz. Juice from tuna fish can
Cottage cheese

Add gin and tuna fish juice to shot glass. Sprinkle in some cottage cheese curds and serve.

SMOKING MARTINI

Difficulty Level: 1
Disgust Level: 2

1 1/4 oz. Gin
1/4 oz. Rye
Maraschino cherry

Add ingredients to a cocktail shaker filled with ice. Shake well. Strain into martini glass, garnish with a cherry and serve.

STILTON

Difficulty Level: 1
Disgust Level: 2

1 oz. Gin
1 oz. Milk

Add ingredients to a shot glass and serve.

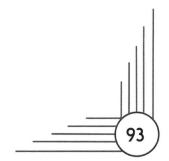

THE AVIATION COCKTAIL
Difficulty Level: 3
Disgust Level: 3

1 1/2 oz. Gin
3/4 oz. Lemon juice
2 dashed Maraschino Liqueur
2 dashes Crème de Violette

Add ingredients to cocktail shaker filled with ice. Shake well. Strain into martini glass. Garnish with maraschino cherry and lemon peel and serve.

THE DEATH RAY
Difficulty Level: 2
Disgust Level: 2

1 oz. Gin
1 oz. Orange juice
1 oz. Mountain Dew

Add ingredients to a rocks glass filled with ice. Stir and serve.

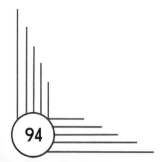

RUM

← →

FAT

Difficulty Level: 2
Disgust Level: 1

1 oz. Coffee liqueur
1 oz. Caramel rum
1 oz. White rum
1/2 oz. Hazelnut syrup
1/2 oz. White chocolate creamer

Add first three ingredients to cocktail shaker filled with ice. Shake. Strain into a martini glass. Drizzle hazelnut syrup and top with white chocolate creamer and serve.

FIRE IN HEAVEN

Difficulty Level: 1
Disgust Level: 3

1 oz. Bacardi 151 Proof Rum
1 dash Hot sauce

Add rum to shot glass. Add hot sauce and allow it to settle and serve.

FIRE IN THE HOLE

Difficulty Level: 1
Disgust Level: 2

1 1/2 oz. Overproof rum
1 dash of grenadine

Add ingredients to shot glass and serve.

FLAMING 151

Difficulty Level: 1
Disgust Level: 1

1 1/2 oz. Overproof Rum

Add rum to shot glass. Light with match and serve.

FRIED CHICKEN
Difficulty Level: 2
Disgust Level: 3

3/4 oz. Bacardi 151 Proof Rum
3/4 oz. Ouzo
1 raw Egg

Add ouzo to glass. Crack and add raw egg without breaking yolk. Top with rum and serve.

GORILLA FART
Difficulty Level: 2
Disgust Level: 3

3/4 oz. Rum
3/4 oz. Bourbon

Add bourbon to shot glass. Carefully layer rum over the top of the bourbon by gently pouring over a spoon and serve.

GREEN LIZARD
Difficulty Level: 1
Disgust Level: 2

1 oz. Overproof Rum
1 oz. Green Chartreuse

Add ingredients to shot glass and serve.

HOT I CAN'T BELIEVE IT'S NOT BUTTERED RUM
Difficulty Level: 2
Disgust Level: 2

2 oz. Malibu Rum
4 oz. Water
1 Tbsp. I Can't Believe It's Not Butter

Add rum and water to mug and warm in microwave. Add I Can't Believe It's Not Butter and stir until dissolved and serve.

LA WATER

Difficulty Level: 2
Disgust Level: 2

1/2 oz. Blue Curacao
1/2 oz. Melon liqueur
1/2 oz. Raspberry liqueur
1 oz. White rum
1 oz. Vodka
splash 7-up
splash Cranberry juice

Add ingredients to pint glass filled with ice. Stir and serve.

LIQUID STEAK

Difficulty Level: 1
Disgust Level: 3

1 oz. Rum
1 oz. Worcestershire sauce

Let the Worcestershire sauce settle before shooting. It'll hit the bottom but kind of disperse through the rum.

MAC AND CHEESE JELLO SHOT

Difficulty Level: 4
Disgust Level: 4

Cheese Rum
Instant Macaroni and cheese (may need milk and butter)
Unflavored Gelatin

Prepare macaroni and cheese and allow it to cool. Add a spoonful to 2-ounce plastic cups. Prepare gelatin according to directions. Instead of adding 1 cup of cold water to Gelatin when it is called for, add 1 cup of rum. Stir until mixed and pour into 2-ounce cups over macaroni and cheese. Put in refrigerator to set and cool. Once cool, serve.

HAM DAIQUIRI

Difficulty Level: 2
Disgust Level: 2

2 oz. Myer's Dark Rum
4 oz. Pineapple juice
1/2 tsp. Liquid smoke
Honey
Cube of ham

Add first four ingredients to cocktail shaker filled with ice.
Shake well. Strain into highball glass with ice. Garnish with
ham.

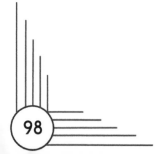

PINK FUZZY MOTHERFUCKER

Difficulty Level: 1
Disgust Level: 2

1 oz. Overproof Rum
2 oz. Peach schnapps
splash Grenadine

Add ingredients to cocktail shaker filled with ice. Shake well. Strain into rocks glass over ice and serve.

PRISON SEX

Difficulty Level: 1
Disgust Level: 3

3/4 oz. Overproof rum
3/4 oz. Absolut Peppar
Louisiana hot sauce

Add ingredients to shot glass. Add 1-2 dashes of hot sauce and serve.

SALMON COLADA

Difficulty Level: 3
Disgust Level: 3

3 oz. Light rum
3 Tbsp. Pineapple juice
3 Tbsp. Coconut milk
1 oz. Raw fresh Atlantic salmon diced as fine as possible
Salmon head

Add first five ingredients to cocktail shaker filled with ice. Shake well. Strain into glass with crushed ice. Garnish with salmon head and serve.

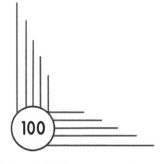

THE BATH CURE
Difficulty Level: 3
Disgust Level: 3

2 oz. Light rum
1/2 oz. Grenadine
1/2 oz. Lime juice
1 1/2 oz. Brandy
1 1/2 oz. Dark rum
1 1/2 oz. Vodka
1 oz. Golden rum
1 oz. Lemon juice
1 oz. Orange juice
1 oz. Bacardi 151 Proof Rum
1 oz. Pineapple juice
1 tsp Simple syrup
lime slice
Maraschino cherry
Red blue, and green food coloring

Mix all ingredients, except lime slice and cherry, with cracked ice in a blender and strain into a 14 or 16 ounce double Old Fashioned-style glass that has been frozen in a mold of shaved ice. Decorate sides of ice mold with red, blue, and green food coloring. Garnish with lime slice and maraschino cherry and serve with two straws.

THE D-BOMB
Difficulty Level: 3
Disgust Level: 4

6 oz. Vodka
6 oz. Light rum
4 Limes
1 Durian

Slice durian in half and scoop out meat. Add to blender with vodka and rum and ice. Add juice from limes. Blend well. Pour into durian halves. Serve with straws.

TOMATO DAIQUIRI

Difficulty Level: 2
Disgust Level: 2

2 oz. Rum
1 oz. Fresh lime juice
1 oz. Simple syrup
1 tsp. Tomato puree
1 dash Angostura bitters

Add ingredients to cocktail shaker filled with ice. Shake
well. Pour into glass and serve.

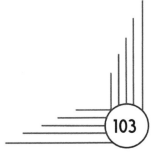

THE D-BOMB

Difficulty Level: 3
Disgust Level: 4

6 oz. Vodka
6 oz. Light rum
4 Limes
1 Durian

Slice durian in half and scoop out meat. Add to blender with vodka and rum and ice. Add juice from limes. Blend well. Pour into durian halves. Serve with straws.

TOMBSTONE

Difficulty Level: 1
Disgust Level: 3

1/2 oz. Overproof Rum
1/2 oz. Goldschläger
1/2 oz. Southern Comfort

Add ingredients to shot glass and serve.

VULCAN MIND PROBE

Difficulty Level: 2
Disgust Level: 2

1/2 oz. Overproof Rum
1/2 oz. Ouzo

Add ingredients to shot glass and serve.

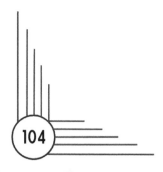

BRANDY

DRUNK, DIRTY AND DISGUSTING

Difficulty Level: 1
Disgust Level: 1

1 oz. Cognac
1 oz. Grand Marnier
1/2 oz. Southern Comfort

Add ingredients to rocks glass filled with ice. Stir and serve.

GOAT'S DELIGHT

Difficulty Level: 3
Disgust Level: 3

1/2 oz. Kirschwasser
1/2 oz. Brandy
1 Tbsp. Cream
dash Orgeat syrup
dash of Absinthe

Add ingredients to cocktail shaker filled with ice. Shake well. Strain into cocktail glass and serve.

NIKOLASCHKA

Difficulty Level: 2
Disgust Level: 1

1 1/2 oz. Cognac
1 tsp. Powdered coffee
1 tsp. Powdered sugar
Lemon disk, peeled

Add cognac to brandy snifter and place the lemon disk on top. Cover half of the disk with powdered coffee and the other half with powdered sugar and serve.

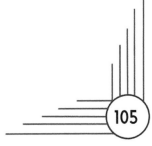

THUNDER

Difficulty Level: 2
Disgust Level: 4

1 1/2 oz. Brandy
1 tsp. powdered sugar
pinch Cayenne pepper
1 Raw egg yolk

Add brandy and sugar to glass. Top with egg yolk. Add
dash of cayenne pepper to egg yolk and serve.

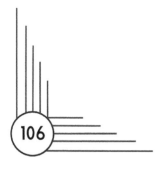

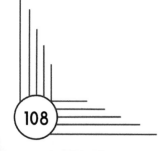

OTHER

AGENT ORANGE

Difficulty Level: 2
Disgust Level: 4

3/4 oz. Everclear
3/4 oz. Tang

Add ingredients to shot glass and serve.
Note: Also called a Buzzed Aldrin.

ATTEMPTED MANSLAUGHTER

Difficulty Level: 2
Disgust Level: 4

3/4 oz. Everclear
1/4 oz. Hot sauce

Add ingredients to shot glass and serve.

CALIMOCHO

Difficulty Level: 1
Disgust Level: 2

4 oz. Red wine
4 oz. Coca Cola

Add ingredients to glass filled with ice. Stir and serve.

DEAD MAN WALKING

Difficulty Level: 2
Disgust Level: 3

1/2 oz. Absinthe
1/2 oz. Goldschläger

Add ingredients to shot glass and serve.

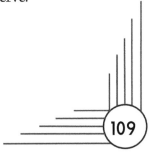

BLACK SAMURAI

Difficulty Level: 1
Disgust Level: 4

1 oz. Sake
1/2 oz. Soy sauce

Add ingredients to shot glass and serve.

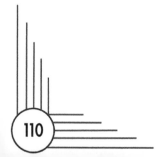

DEATH IN THE AFTERNOON

Difficulty Level: 2
Disgust Level: 2

1 1/2 oz. Absinthe
4 1/2 oz. Champagne, chilled

Add ingredients to a champagne flute and serve.

ENPINYO AND COW BLOOD

Difficulty Level: 5
Disgust Level: 5

2 oz. Enpinyo (distilled African liquor)
2 oz. Fresh cow blood

Add ingredients to a glass and serve.

FISH WATER

Difficulty Level: 1
Disgust Level: 3

2 oz. Jägermeister
2 oz. Orange juice

Add ingredients to rocks glass filled with ice. Stir and serve.

NEW JERSEY TURNPIKE

Difficulty Level: 5
Disgust Level: 5

1 Bar mat
1 Bar rag

Ask the bartender to empty the contents of the bar mat into a glass. Then ask the bartender to wring the bar rag into the glass and serve.

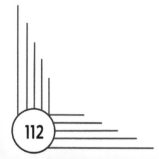

REDNECK PRAIRIE FIRE

Difficulty Level: 2
Disgust Level: 2

1 oz. Moonshine
1/4 oz. Louisiana hot sauce

Add ingredients to shot glass and serve.

THE HIROSHIMA

Difficulty Level: 2
Disgust Level: 3

1 1/2 oz. Sake
Cigarette Ash

Add sake to shot glass. Top with cigarette ash and serve.

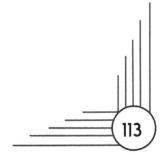

ABOUT THE AUTHORS

Clint Lanier and Derek Hembree are the authors of the book, Drunken History, and of the best-selling travel guide, Bucket List Bars: Historic Saloons, Pubs and Dives of America. To write their guide they travelled the U.S. for almost a decade, going to the oldest bars in the country's biggest cities, interviewing bartenders, owners, and patrons, and leaving a sea of empty cocktail glasses in their wake. When not traveling or researching for one of their books, Clint teaches writing at New Mexico State University and Derek works in the power industry.

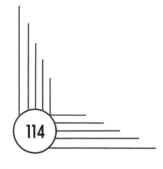

CONNECT WITH US

Questions or comments about the rinks in here? Are we completely, arrogantly wrong about some? Do YOU have a drink we just have to include in the next book? Let us know!

Mail
Craptails
c/o AO Media LLC
2015 Cotton Ave.
Las Cruces, NM 88001

Email
info@craptails.com

Find Us on the Web
http://www.craptails.com

Follow Us on Twitter
@DrunkenHistory
@ClintonRLanier
@DerekHembree

Connect on Facebook
Facebook.com/drunkenhistory

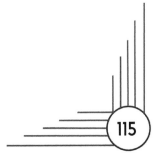

Lightning Source UK Ltd.
Milton Keynes UK
UKHW021524100223
416696UK00001B/29